WOUNDED & LOVING

LIVING WITH TRAUMA AND LOVING SOMEONE WITH TRAUMA

KENZIE KATTICH

To those who carry invisible battles, the ones who wake up each day and choose to keep going, even when the weight of yesterday still lingers, this is for you.

To those who love someone living with trauma, who stay even when understanding feels impossible, this is for you, too.

To my brothers and sisters in uniform, past and present, the ones who have seen too much, felt too deeply, and kept serving anyway, may you find peace in knowing that healing is not weakness. It is courage in its truest form.

To my son, Bryson, you are the reason I choose healing every day. I promise to do everything in my power to ensure you never have to carry the pain your parents once did. May you grow up knowing safety, peace, and love that does not have to be earned. You are proof that the cycle can end, and that new beginnings are possible.

And to my therapist, I get it now.

ACKNOWLEDGEMENTS

This book was born from the stories that shaped me, my own, and those of the people I've had the privilege to walk beside.

To my fellow veterans and first responders who live with trauma: thank you for your service, your honesty, and your resilience. The strength it takes to face trauma, and to speak about it, is the strength that changes lives.

To my friends and loved ones who live with trauma: your stories have taught me more about compassion, patience, and hope than any classroom ever could. Thank you for trusting me with your truths.

To every reader who has ever felt broken, misunderstood, or "too much", may these pages remind you that you are not alone, and that healing is not a destination, but a return to yourself.

Finally, to the quiet moments, the ones spent in reflection, prayer, or silence, that taught me that stillness is strength and vulnerability is power.

Thank you for being part of this journey.

RECOMMENDED PLAYLIST

Part I: The Unraveling

(Chapters 1–5: Understanding Trauma, Hidden Wounds, and Self-Awareness)

1. "The Night We Met", Lord Huron

2. "Liability", Lorde

3. "Creep", Radiohead (Acoustic version)

4. "Stone Cold", Demi Lovato

5. "Breathe Me", Sia

6. "The Archer", Taylor Swift

7. "Skinny Love", Bon Iver

Part II: The Reckoning

(Chapters 6–10: Safety, Trust, and Loving While Healing)

1. "Hold On", Adele

2. "Let It Go", James Bay

3. "Saturn", Sleeping at Last

4. "Someone New", Hozier

5. "Unsteady", X Ambassadors

6.	"You Say", Lauren Daigle

Part III: The Mirror

(Chapters 11–15: Triggers, Communication, and Codependency)

1.	"Elastic Heart (Piano Version)", Sia

2.	"Love Me Still", Chaka Khan

3.	"Cannonball", Damien Rice

4.	"Chasing Cars", Snow Patrol

5.	"Good Thing", Kehlani

6.	"Let It Hurt", Rascal Flatts

Part IV: The Healing

(Chapters 16–18: Trauma-Informed Love, Mutual Healing, and When Love Isn't Enough)

1.	"Conversations in the Dark", John Legend

2.	"Beyond", Leon Bridges

3.	"Work Song", Hozier

4.	"From the Ground Up", Dan + Shay

5.	"Love Like Ghosts", Lord Huron

6.	"All My Days", Alexi Murdoch

7.	"Lease On Life", Andy Grammer

Part V: The Becoming

(Chapters 19–20: Integration, Wholeness, and Hope After the Wound)

1.   "Rainbow", Kacey Musgraves

2.   "Rise Up", Andra Day

3.   "Brighter Days", Blessing Offor

4.   "Dog Days Are Over", Florence + The Machine

5.   "Undefeated", Daughtry

6.   "Shake It Out", Florence + The Machine

7.   "Unwritten", Natasha Bedingfield

8.   "Bigger Than The Whole Sky", Taylor Swift

Bonus: For the Nights You Need to Feel It All

(Because sometimes you just need to cry, journal, or lie still in the glow of your own becoming.)

- "Let It All Go", Birdy & Rhodes

- "Slow Dancing in a Burning Room", John Mayer

- "Liability (Reprise)", Lorde

- "Never Be Mine", Angel Olsen

- "In My Veins", Andrew Belle

Bonus: Don't Forget to Dance and Sing Off Key

- "Mr. Brightside", The Killers

- "Ain't It Fun", Paramore

- "I Wanna Dance With Somebody (Who Loves Me)", Whitney Houston

- "Love myself" – Hailey Steinfeld

- "Good as Hell", Lizzo

- "Firework", Katy Perry

Contents

PART I: THE UNRAVELLING 1

Chapter 1: What Trauma Really Is? 3

Chapter 2: Hidden Trauma 8

Chapter 3: Intergenerational Trauma 16

Chapter 4: Why It's Not "Just in the Past" 23

Chapter 5: When You Are the One Carrying Trauma 29

Chapter 6: Re-learning Safety 37

PART II: THE RECKONING......................41

Chapter 7: Trusting Yourself Again 43

Chapter 8: The Exhaustion of Healing..................... 49

Chapter 9: Loving While Healing 56

Chapter 10: When It's Hard to Love Someone Who's Been Hurt 60

PART III: THE MIRROR 63

Chapter 11: Emotional Inconsistency and the Nervous System's Alarm 65

Chapter 12: Triggers in Daily Life........................ 70

Chapter 13: Communication That Doesn't Trigger.... 83

Chapter 14: When They Push You Away 91

Chapter 15: Codependency vs. Compassion 96

Part IV: The Healing 103

Chapter 16: Building a Trauma-Informed Relationship 105

Chapter 17: When Both of You Have Trauma........ 112

Chapter 18: When Love Isn't Enough..................... 119

Part V: The Becoming.............................. 123

Chapter 19: The Myth of the "Healed" Person........ 125

Chapter 20: Hope After the Wound 133

Epilogue: You Made It Here.................................. 138

Resource Appendix 141

PART I:
THE UNRAVELLING

Chapter 1: What Trauma Really Is?

Trauma isn't just what *happened* to you. It's what happened *inside* you because of what you went through.

It's the body's and brain's long-lasting response to experiences that felt unsafe, uncontrollable, or simply too much to handle at the time, emotionally or physically.

Now, when people hear the word *"trauma,"* they often picture car accidents, war zones, or dramatic movie scenes scored with violins. But trauma isn't defined by how big or cinematic an event was, it's defined by how *alone and unsafe* you felt when it happened.

Two people can live through the same situation, a house fire, a breakup, a critical parent, and come out with completely different scars. One might shake it off after a good cry and a pint of ice cream; the other might find their nervous system goes into panic at the faintest whiff of smoke or conflict.

The difference isn't strength, it's *support and safety*. Trauma isn't in the event itself; it's in the *absence of enough safety to process it.*

Types of Trauma (Because Apparently There's More Than One Kind)

- **Acute Trauma:** The "one big event" kind, a car accident, an assault, an IED blowing up your convoy, a sudden loss. It's the emotional equivalent of getting caught in a thunderstorm without an umbrella.

- **Complex Trauma:** The "it kept happening" kind, ongoing abuse, neglect, deployments, or constant chaos. This one doesn't strike once; it slowly erodes your sense of safety over time.

- **Developmental Trauma:** The "I didn't even know that counted" kind, which occurs in childhood when your brain and body are still developing for life. It's not always caused by obvious harm but often by what was *missing*: emotional warmth, consistency, and being truly seen.

Each type can shape how you interpret the world, how quickly you sense danger, how easily you trust, and how much safety you believe you deserve.

The Nervous System's Role: Your Inner Security Guard (Who Never Sleeps)

Your nervous system is basically your body's alarm system and emotional security guard, constantly scanning your environment and asking one question: *"Am I safe?"*

When it senses danger, it pulls the fire alarm, triggering fight, flight, freeze, or fawn. These are your body's automatic survival responses. They're not personality flaws; they're built-in safety features. (Think of them as the emergency exits of your nervous system, not glamorous, but effective.)

The tricky part? After trauma, the alarm doesn't always reset. It can get stuck in the "on" position, even long after the danger has passed. That's why your heart races at a harmless sound or why a certain tone of voice makes your stomach drop. Your body is still trying to protect you, it just hasn't realized that the threat is over.

Why Healing Isn't Just "Thinking Positive"

You can't logic your way out of trauma because trauma doesn't live in logic. It lives in your muscles, your breath, your pulse, and your gut.

That's why real healing isn't just about changing your thoughts, it's about helping your body feel safe again. It's learning to tell your nervous system, gently and repeatedly: *"It's okay now. You're safe to rest."*

So if you've ever felt like you "should be over it by now," remember, your body is just taking its time to believe what your mind already knows:

The danger has passed.

You made it through.

And safety, though it may take a while, is something you can feel again.

If this is you... (for trauma survivors):

You might not think of what you went through as "trauma," but something inside you still feels unsettled. Maybe you flinch at raised voices, struggle to trust, or feel on edge even when nothing's wrong. You're not weak or broken; your body has learned to stay alert to survive. This chapter will help you understand why and remind you that what happened *inside you* matters as much as what happened to you.

If this is you... (for loved ones):

If someone you care about seems distant, guarded, or easily triggered, it doesn't mean they don't trust you; it means their body hasn't felt safe in a long time. Trauma changes how a person experiences the world. Your patience, curiosity, and calm presence can help them start to feel safe again.

Chapter 2:
Hidden Trauma

Not all trauma comes crashing into your life with sirens and chaos.

Some kinds slip in quietly, like a draft through a cracked window.

Hidden trauma doesn't always come from what was done to you.

Sometimes it's what wasn't.

It's the missing warmth, the unspoken affection, the moments when no one noticed you were hurting.

It's growing up in a home where your basic needs were met, but your emotional ones were quietly ignored, like someone forgot to water the plant and then wondered why it wilted.

You learned to silence your feelings before you even learned to name them. You taught yourself to shrink your needs, to believe that being "too emotional" made you hard to love.

This kind of trauma doesn't leave visible scars.

However, it leaves patterns in how you love, how you talk to yourself, and how safe you feel simply by being who you are.

Emotional Neglect:

The Invisible Disconnection

Emotional neglect is the silence between words.

It's the parent who's physically present but emotionally tuned to another frequency, one where your feelings don't quite register.

They might never have yelled, hit, or left.

They just didn't see you.

Over time, your brain learns that emotions are messy, inconvenient, maybe even dangerous. You begin to disconnect from your inner world, a kind of quiet self-abandonment you don't even notice happening.

As adults, this can look like:

- Feeling numb instead of sad.

- Downplaying pain because "other people had it worse."

- Becoming hyper-independent, the human equivalent of "it's fine, I'll carry all the groceries in one trip."

The truth is that emotional neglect doesn't erase your emotions.

It just teaches you to hide them, even from yourself, like tucking away a secret you're not sure anyone would care to hear.

Chronic Invalidation: The Subtle Shaming of Feelings

"You're overreacting."

"It wasn't that bad."

"Stop being so sensitive."

Sound familiar? These phrases might seem harmless, but repeated over time, they deliver a message loud and clear: *your feelings are wrong*.

Chronic invalidation slowly trains you to distrust your inner world.

You start to wonder:

- Am I making this up?

- Was it really that bad?

- Maybe I am too sensitive.

The wound isn't just in the dismissal, it's in the confusion that follows.

You stop believing your own emotional compass. You start outsourcing your reality, waiting for someone else to tell you if your pain "counts."

But here's the truth (and you can write this one down somewhere):

Your emotions don't need external approval.

They are real, simply because you feel them.

(And yes, you can quote me when someone says you're "too sensitive." Tell them you're just emotionally literate.)

The Invisible Wounds

People with hidden trauma often look like they have it all together.

They're the caregivers, the achievers, the ones who smile and say, "I'm fine", even when their soul is quietly waving a white flag.

They often seem composed, maybe even thriving.

But inside, there's an ache that success can't soothe.

Invisible wounds can show up as:

- Chronic self-doubt or perfectionism.

- Feeling detached from joy.

- A deep sense of loneliness, even when surrounded by people.

- Numbness that masquerades as calm.

These aren't flaws. They're adaptations.

You learned to survive by minimizing your needs, and it worked.

But now that survival mode is no longer needed, it's keeping you from fully living.

Recognizing It in Yourself

Hidden trauma rarely introduces itself with a dramatic entrance. It's more subtle, like background music you didn't realize was playing all along.

You might notice it in small, everyday ways:

- Apologizing for existing.

- Staying quiet to avoid conflict.

- Feeling guilty for resting, asking for help, or just being.

- Saying "yes" when you want to say "no."

- Constantly checking if others are upset with you (spoiler: they usually aren't).

If this sounds familiar, please know, this doesn't mean you're broken.

It means you adapted.

And now, you have permission to unlearn survival and learn safety instead.

The Healing Work

Healing hidden trauma starts with acknowledgment.

You cannot heal what you continue to dismiss.

Start small, healing doesn't have to look like fireworks and breakthroughs. Sometimes it's a whisper: *I matter, too.*

Try this:

- **Validate your feelings.** When something hurts, say to yourself, "This makes sense." (Not "I shouldn't feel this way." You should, because you do.)

- **Practice emotional presence.** Feel what you feel, no fixing, no explaining, just witnessing.

- **Reparent your inner child.** Offer yourself the comfort you once needed: "I see you. You're allowed to feel this."

- **Reconnect with your needs.** Rest, affection, boundaries, these aren't indulgences; they're basic human fuel.

Over time, the silence you grew up with turns into compassion.

Self-doubt softens into trust.

Emptiness makes room for belonging.

The Heart of It All

Just because your pain wasn't visible doesn't mean it wasn't real.

Hidden trauma counts. And it deserves healing, too.

You are not "too much."

You were simply made to believe you had to be less.

Now, you get to reclaim all the space you were always worthy of, and maybe take a deep, unapologetic breath while you're at it.

Chapter 3:
Intergenerational Trauma

Trauma doesn't always begin with you.

Sometimes, it begins generations before, carried silently through survival, passed down through unspoken fears, and inherited through the ways people love, protect, and withdraw.

Families transmit more than eye color or bone structure.

They pass down beliefs about safety, emotions, and worthiness.

The echoes of unhealed pain can live in our nervous systems, shaping how we react, relate, and recover, even when we can't trace the origin of our feelings.

You may be living out a story that started long before you were born.

Emotional Inheritance: The Weight You Didn't Choose

Your parents may not have intended to pass down their pain, but pain has its own language.

It speaks through silence, fear, control, and avoidance.

A mother who grew up in chaos may teach her child that emotions are dangerous.

A father who was never nurtured may struggle to offer tenderness.

A grandparent who survived war or poverty may instill hypervigilance as love: "Always be ready."

You inherit not just their genes, but their *emotional DNA*, their survival responses, their unresolved grief, and their mistrust of safety.

When they say, "we did our best," it's often true.

But "our best" can still carry harm when it's shaped by unhealed wounds.

Recognizing this isn't blame, it's clarity. And clarity is where healing begins.

Family Survival Scripts: The Rules You Were Raised On

Every family has its scripts, unwritten rules that quietly govern belonging.

They often sound like:

- "We don't talk about that."

- "Be strong."

- "Don't make it harder for everyone else."

- "Keep the peace."

These scripts once served a purpose. They kept families functioning through hardship, shame, or scarcity. But what helps a family *survive* can prevent its members from *healing*.

You may have learned to silence your feelings to protect others.

You may have been rewarded for self-denial or punished for honesty. Breaking these rules can feel like betrayal, but it's actually loyalty to truth.

To heal intergenerational trauma, you must be willing to write new scripts. Ones that say:

- "We can talk about it."

- "It's okay to feel."

- "Love doesn't require silence."

Attachment Transmission: How Love Gets Inherited

Attachment isn't just about childhood; it's a pattern that travels through generations.

How your caregivers relate to you becomes your internal blueprint for love. If they were emotionally distant, you may equate closeness with danger. If they were unpredictable, you may confuse intensity with connection. If they were nurturing, you may carry a sense of security that ripples outward.

This is how love becomes generational, both its abundance and its absence.

When you notice your own attachment patterns, you're decoding your family's emotional history. You start to see that your difficulty with trust, fear of abandonment, or need for control isn't a flaw; it's an inheritance. *And you have the power to stop it here.*

Breaking the Pattern: Awareness as Rebellion

Awareness is the first act of rebellion.

To see what was once unseen is to interrupt generations of silence.

When you say, "This ends with me," you're not dishonoring your family; you're honoring the parts of them that never got the chance to heal.

Breaking the pattern looks like:

• Choosing communication over avoidance.

• Setting boundaries even when it feels unfamiliar.

• Allowing softness in a lineage that valued strength above all else.

You become the bridge between what was and what can be.

Healing Forward: Writing a New Emotional Legacy

Healing intergenerational trauma isn't about erasing the past; it's about transforming your relationship to it.

You can't rewrite what happened, but you can choose what continues.

You can grieve for what your parents never received.

You can offer compassion without carrying their burdens.

You can model to your own children, partners, or loved ones what safety feels like, not by perfection, but by presence.

Healing forward means creating a new kind of inheritance: An inheritance of honesty, softness, and self-trust.

You might not be responsible for what hurt you, but you are powerful enough to stop it from continuing.

Your healing is not selfish; it's generational repair.

When you tend to your own wounds, you free the future from repeating the past.

Chapter 4:
Why It's Not "Just in the Past"

People love to say things like, *"That was years ago. Why can't you just move on?"* (Usually said by someone who still brings up what their coworker did in 2014.)

But trauma doesn't live in the calendar.

It lives in the body.

It's not just a memory filed neatly in your brain like an old photo; it's more like an alarm system that got stuck in the "on" position. Your nervous system remembers the feeling of danger, even when your mind insists everything's fine.

A sound, a smell, a tone of voice, even a sideways glance, any of these can act like a time machine, pulling your body back to a moment it never got to safely leave.

Your heart races, your muscles tense, your breath shortens, and logic quietly slips out the back door.

Because to your nervous system, danger isn't over yet.

When Your Body Still Thinks It's in the Past

Trauma can make ordinary life feel unpredictable. You might find yourself over-preparing for small things ("just in case"), avoiding certain people or places, or scanning the room like your brain moonlights as a security guard. Did I mention I refuse to sit with my back to the entrance when I go out to eat? Yeah, I do it too.

And while it can feel frustrating, these aren't signs of weakness; they're signs of protection.

Your body is doing its best to keep you safe using the tools it learned a long time ago.

Even when your *mind* knows you're safe, your *body* might still be checking the exits.

A Simple Example (and a Small Moment of Compassion)

Imagine someone hearing a car backfire. For most people, it's just an annoying noise. For me, it's an invitation to say, "wow, he must have a huge d*ck".

For someone with trauma, though, that sound might send their body into a full survival response: heart pounding, muscles clenching, adrenaline firing.

They might duck, freeze, or suddenly feel panic rise from nowhere. The mind knows it's now. But the body still thinks it's *then*.

That's what trauma does: it keeps you ready for a danger that's already passed.

The good news? Your body isn't betraying you. It's trying (a little too hard) to protect you.

What Healing Really Means

Healing isn't about erasing what happened or pretending it didn't hurt.

It's about gently teaching your body and mind that *this moment, right now, is safe.*

It's not a switch you flip; it's a language you learn.

You teach safety through small, consistent experiences:

- Noticing a slow breath.

- Feeling the weight of your body on a chair.

- Letting yourself laugh and realizing, even for a second, that you're okay.

Over time, these moments add up.

Your nervous system starts to learn that it can relax without letting its guard down completely.

Healing is basically the process of helping your body update its software: *The threat is over. You survived. It's safe to rest now.*

You don't have to "just move on."

You're already moving, gently, courageously, every time you breathe through a moment your body once feared.

And that's not a weakness.

That's wisdom learned through survival.

If this is you… (for trauma survivors)

You might notice moments when your body reacts before your mind understands why. Maybe your chest tightens during an argument, or you suddenly feel distant in a situation that should feel normal. Maybe certain sights, sounds, or smells bring back memories you thought were long gone. You're not "overreacting"; your nervous system is doing its best to protect you. Healing begins when you pause, breathe, and remind yourself: *I'm safe now.* Over time, your body will gradually learn to trust the present, rather than just remembering the past.

If this is you… (for loved ones)

If someone you care about seems to "shut down" or "overreact" to something small, remember that their response isn't about the present moment; it's about the past their body hasn't realized is over. Their reactions are automatic, not intentional. Your calm presence, gentle tone, and patience can help their nervous system re-learn what safety feels like.

Sometimes, the most healing thing you can do is simply stay grounded while they find their footing.

Chapter 5:
When You Are the One Carrying Trauma

Some days, healing feels like carrying invisible luggage. You can't see it, but you know it's there, because even joy feels heavy.

Learning to recognize the weight you've been holding, and to put some of it down.

Carrying trauma can feel like walking through life with an invisible backpack full of bricks; you can't always explain why you're so tired, but you know you're carrying something heavy.

It doesn't always show up as vivid memories or nightmares. Sometimes it shows up in quieter ways:

in how you apologize too much,

overthink a simple text,

or freeze when someone raises their voice.

Trauma can live not only in your past, but in your patterns, how you love, how you cope, how you see yourself.

And the tricky part? You might not even realize you're carrying it. You just think, *"Why am I like this?"*

But what if the answer is, *"Because you survived something that changed you"*?

Feeling "Too Much" or "Not Enough"

Trauma has a way of distorting the mirror we see ourselves in.

Some days, you might feel like you're *too much*, too sensitive, too emotional, too complicated. Other days, you feel *not enough*, not strong enough, not interesting enough, not worthy enough.

It's a confusing loop: one moment you're worried you take up too much space, the next you're afraid you don't deserve any.

But here's the truth: both of these feelings come from the same root, the nervous system trying to protect you from rejection.

When you once felt unsafe, you learned to shrink or overcompensate to stay connected. Maybe you dimmed your light to avoid attention, or amplified your caretaking to earn love. These aren't flaws; they're adaptations.

So, when those "too much" or "not enough" moments come up, try whispering this reminder to yourself: *My sensitivity is not a flaw. It's a sign that I feel deeply. And my worth doesn't disappear when I'm quiet.*

Also, for the record, "too many" people are often exactly the right amount; it's just that some environments were too small to hold them.

Self-Sabotage and Shame Cycles

Let's talk about self-sabotage, that mysterious force that convinces you to avoid the thing you actually want.

You might procrastinate on the project that matters most.

Or ghost the person who makes you feel seen.

Or freeze right before you take a leap that could change everything.

Then comes the shame spiral: *"Why do I keep doing this to myself?"*

Here's why: your nervous system doesn't care about your dreams; it cares about your *safety*. And sometimes, success, intimacy, or visibility feels unsafe when all you've ever known is struggle.

So self-sabotage isn't laziness, it's self-protection wearing the wrong outfit.

The healing work here isn't about forcing yourself to "just do it." It's about gently showing your body that it's safe to have good things now. You can start by noticing the pattern without attacking yourself for it.

Awareness breaks the spell; compassion rewires it.

And when you find yourself mid-spiral, try saying, *"Okay, nervous system, I see what you're doing. Thank you for trying to keep me safe. But we're okay now."*

(It sounds silly, but your body actually listens.)

Emotional Flashbacks: When the Past Crashes the Present

Unlike a memory that sits quietly in your mind, an emotional flashback hijacks the whole show.

You're having a normal day, and then someone raises their voice, or you smell a familiar scent, and suddenly your body reacts like it's 10 years ago. Your heart races, your chest tightens, and part of you feels small, scared, or enraged.

Meanwhile, your adult mind is standing there like, *"What just happened?"*

This is your body reliving an old experience it never got to finish. It's not weakness or overreaction; it's a nervous system time warp.

When this happens, the goal isn't to fight it, but to name it.

Try saying quietly to yourself: *"This is an emotional flashback. It's not happening now."*

Then use grounding tools to bring yourself back:

- Feel your feet on the floor.

- Name five things you can see.

- Take a slow breath out, longer than your inhale.

Each small act of grounding is a message to your body: *"The danger is over. You're safe here."*

And over time, those messages add up. Your nervous system learns that it doesn't have to hit the panic button every time it recognizes an old pattern.

The Gentle Truth

Carrying trauma doesn't mean you're broken; it means your body and mind have learned how to protect you, even if those methods have outlived their usefulness.

You don't have to "get over it." You just have to get closer to your own story, your own body, your own compassion.

The weight of trauma lightens not when you drop it all at once, but when you learn you were never meant to carry it alone.

So, take a breath. Adjust the backpack. Maybe even set it down for a while.

You're not behind in your healing; you're just human.

And that's more than enough.

If this is you… (for trauma survivors)

You might notice patterns in your life that leave you feeling stuck, moments when you feel "too much" or "not enough," or when you push yourself away from opportunities and people you care about. Emotional flashbacks may appear unexpectedly, leaving you feeling confused, tense, or afraid. You're not failing or broken; your body and nervous system are responding to past danger. Healing begins when you pause, notice these patterns without judgment, and remind yourself: *I am safe now.*

If this is you… (for loved ones)

If someone you care about seems to self-sabotage, withdraw, or react strongly to small triggers, it's not about you; it's about their body and mind responding to past experiences. Your patience, calm presence, and gentle support can help them feel seen and safe. Sometimes simply staying grounded and compassionate while they navigate these moments is the most healing thing you can do.

Chapter 6:
Re-learning Safety

After trauma, your nervous system has been on high alert for a long time. Even in completely safe moments, your body may act as if danger is lurking.

Re-learning safety is about gently teaching yourself, body and mind, that it's okay to relax, that the present moment is not a threat.

Take it one breath at a time. One step at a time.

You are learning, and every small step counts.

Grounding Techniques

Grounding brings you back to the present moment, reminding your body that you are safe.

It can be as simple as noticing the feeling of your feet on the floor, holding a warm cup of tea, or taking a deep, slow breath.

Try the 5-4-3-2-1 technique: name five things you can see, four you can touch, three you can hear, two you can smell, and one you can taste.

You are here. You are safe. You are enough.

Internal Self-Talk and Co-Regulation

Your inner dialogue matters. Words can calm your nervous system or fuel fear. Try gentle phrases like: *"I am safe right now," "It's okay to feel this,"* or *"I am doing my best, and that is enough."*

Co-regulation is learning to feel safe with others. When someone you trust stays calm and present while you feel upset, your body learns that you can survive strong emotions.

Safety is possible. Support is available. You are not alone.

Reparenting and Inner Child Work

Trauma can leave parts of you feeling small, scared, or unworthy. Reparenting is the act of giving those parts the care, reassurance, and love they need. You can silently say to yourself, *"I am here for you. You are safe now."* Journaling letters to your inner child or visualizing comforting experiences are ways to remind yourself: *You matter. You are seen. You are loved.*

Remember: healing isn't about rushing or forcing change. It's about small, steady steps that teach your body, your mind, and your heart that it's safe to relax, to feel, to live.

Every breath, every grounding moment, every word of self-kindness is progress. *You are learning to trust life again, and that is beautiful.*

If this is you… (for trauma survivors)

You might notice your body tensing, your mind racing, or your emotions feeling overwhelming even in safe moments. Grounding techniques, like focusing on your breath, noticing your surroundings, or gently moving your body, can help you reconnect to the present. Paying attention to your inner dialogue and offering yourself kind, reassuring words helps your nervous system feel supported.

Reparenting and inner child work give the parts of you that were hurt the care and safety they needed.

Even small practices, like silently telling yourself *"I am safe, and I am here for you"* or journaling to your inner child, can slowly retrain your body and mind to trust safety again.

If this is you... (for loved ones)

If someone you care about struggles with fear, tension, or emotional overwhelm, your calm presence can help regulate their nervous system. Encouraging grounding exercises, listening without judgment, or helping them practice supportive self-talk can make them feel safe and seen. Sometimes, the most healing thing you can do is simply stay present while they re-learn safety.

PART II:
THE RECKONING

Chapter 7:
Trusting Yourself Again

Rebuilding self-trust isn't about certainty; it's about self-loyalty.

When you've been betrayed, dismissed, or made to question your own reality, trust doesn't just break between you and others; it fractures inside you.

You start doubting your instincts.

You apologize for setting boundaries.

You second-guess every decision, wondering if your intuition is just fear wearing a disguise.

Trauma teaches you to survive by staying hyperaware of danger. But survival mode and self-trust cannot coexist. Survival asks, *"Am I safe?"* Self-trust answers, *"I am."*

How Trauma Breaks Self-Trust

Trauma rewires your internal compass.

It teaches your body that safety is unpredictable and that vigilance equals survival.

When your emotions were ignored or invalidated, you learned that your inner world couldn't be trusted.

When betrayal came from someone you depended on, your nervous system encoded confusion as protection.

So, you adapted. You learned to look outward for cues, waiting for others to confirm what's real, what's okay, what's too much.

But every time you override your gut, you reinforce the message: *I can't trust myself.*

Healing begins when you start asking: *What if I do know? What if I always have?*

Differentiating Fear from Intuition

For many trauma survivors, fear and intuition feel identical. Both can come with tension, racing thoughts, or a sense of urgency. But their roots are different.

- Fear is reactive; it comes from the past, from patterns that once kept you safe.

- Intuition is responsive; it arises in the present, grounded and calm, even when it warns you to move away.

A simple distinction: fear shouts; intuition speaks quietly but firmly.

You can begin to tell the difference by pausing before reacting. Ask yourself:

- Is this a flashback or feedback?

- Am I responding to what's happening now, or what happened before?

- Does this feeling want to protect me, or guide me?

Learning to listen with curiosity, not judgment, helps your intuition regain its voice.

Small Acts of Re-Trusting

Self-trust isn't rebuilt through grand declarations; it's restored through small, consistent acts.

Every time you keep a promise to yourself, no matter how small, you send your nervous system a message: *I'm here. I'll listen.*

Start small:

- Notice when you're tired, and rest instead of pushing through.
- Say "no" even if your voice shakes.
- Eat when you're hungry, not just when it's "time."
- Journal your instincts before seeking advice.

These micro-moments of alignment slowly stitch self-trust back together.

You don't need to *feel* confident to begin; you just need to be willing to believe your inner world deserves attention.

Repair Through Consistency

Self-trust grows in repetition, not perfection.

Every time you show up for yourself, gently, reliably, your body learns safety. Over time, consistency becomes evidence: *I can depend on myself.*

Try daily self-attunement rituals:

- Check in with your emotions like you would with a friend: *How am I feeling right now?*

- Name your needs without judgment.

- Celebrate small moments of alignment, finishing a task, resting without guilt, and expressing truth kindly.

Trust doesn't return overnight; it returns through presence.

Consistency is how you teach your nervous system that your body and mind are on the same team again.

Listening to Your Nervous System

Your body has been protecting you all along, even in the moments you felt betrayed by it. The anxiety, the freeze, the shutdown, they were all forms of love in disguise.

Now it's time to rebuild that relationship.

Learn your body's language:

- A tight chest might mean, "Something feels off."

- A sigh might mean, "I'm safe enough to release."

• A surge of energy might be excitement, not danger.

When you honor these signals, you reconnect with the wisdom that trauma once made you doubt.

Your body isn't the enemy of your healing; it's the entry point to it.

You don't have to always be right to know what feels true.

Every moment you choose to listen, to pause, to honor your own signals, you are coming home to yourself.

And that home was never lost. Only forgotten.

Chapter 8:
The Exhaustion of Healing

Let's be honest, healing can feel like a full-time job.

You start out with good intentions: therapy, journaling, breathwork, shadow work, reparenting, inner-child letters, moon rituals, and that one yoga pose that's supposed to unlock generational trauma (spoiler: it mostly unlocks hamstring pain).

And then, somewhere between "mindfulness" and "manifesting your highest self," you realize...

You're exhausted.

Healing was supposed to bring peace, but sometimes it feels like homework that never ends.

There's guilt when you rest, guilt when you don't, guilt when you forget to be "grateful." You begin to wonder if maybe you need a nap more than another affirmation.

Understanding Healing Fatigue

Let's name it: healing fatigue.

It's that bone-deep tiredness that comes from trying so hard to feel better that you forget what "better" even feels like.

When you live in survival mode for years, finally having the space to heal can unleash a wave of pressure. *I have to fix everything now.*

But healing isn't a race; it's more like a slow, scenic walk… with occasional rest stops, snack breaks, and maybe a nap under a tree.

When "Doing the Work" Becomes a Coping Mechanism

At some point, self-improvement can start looking suspiciously like self-punishment in disguise.

You might find yourself thinking:

- *If I can just heal a little faster, I'll finally feel okay.*

• *If I stay busy fixing myself, maybe I won't have to feel this grief.*

But constant "doing" keeps your nervous system in overdrive, the very state you're trying to soothe.

Sometimes, "doing the work" becomes the new way we avoid the stillness that actually heals us.

Because stillness can be terrifying, it's where the feelings live. But it's also where peace begins.

The Weight of Letting Go

Sometimes the exhaustion isn't from all the journaling or therapy, it's from the emotional heaviness of finally walking away.

You can cut someone off for your own peace and still feel the ache of resentment.

You can create distance and still find yourself replaying old conversations in your head.

That resentment is its own kind of fatigue, the weight of still being tethered to what you left behind.

It's hard to admit that even healthy choices can hurt.

You might think *I did the right thing. Why doesn't it feel lighter?*

Resentment begins to loosen its grip when we stop waiting for the past to be different.

Healing isn't about forcing forgiveness or pretending it didn't matter; it's about accepting that it *did* and allowing yourself to stop carrying it.

Sometimes it's not anger that softens the pain, but grief, the quiet mourning of what should have been.

And grief, unlike anger, eventually leads you back to peace.

Permission to Pause

You are allowed to take a break from healing.

Read that again, *slowly*.

Rest is not regression.

Rest is repair.

There's no spiritual points system keeping track of how many hours you've spent in introspection this week. You're not going to lose your "growth badge" if you spend an afternoon watching something ridiculous or napping with your dog.

In fact, sometimes the most healing thing you can do is nothing. Because "nothing" tells your body: *We are safe now.*

In the military, they say, "work smarter, not harder." Healing is no different.

Redefining Progress

Healing isn't linear; it's more like a spiral staircase.

You circle around old lessons, but each time you see them from a higher perspective.

Some days you'll feel strong and centered. Other days, you'll wonder if you've made any progress at all.

That's not failure, that's humanity.

Progress isn't how consistently you feel good; it's how kindly you treat yourself when you don't.

Healing is not about becoming perfect; it's about becoming patient.

Gentle Practices for the Tired Soul

When the work of healing starts to feel heavy, gentleness is medicine.

Try things that don't demand effort, things that invite ease back into your body:

- **Grounding:** Step outside, feel your feet on the earth, and let the ground hold some of your weight.

- **Joy:** Do something that makes you laugh; bad dancing absolutely counts.

- **Embodiment:** Stretch, sway, breathe; let movement be permission, not performance.

- **Connection:** Spend time with people who make you feel like sunlight, not like homework.

Healing doesn't have to be solemn to be sacred.

Sometimes, laughter is the most profound release of all.

So go ahead, close the journal, skip the meditation app this time, and take a nap.

You've done enough for today. And that, too, is healing.

55

Chapter 9:
Loving While Healing

Sounds impossible. I know.

You want closeness, but vulnerability still gives you heartburn.

You crave connection, but sometimes your nervous system just wants to hide under a blanket labeled Do Not Disturb, processing emotions.

If that's you, take a breath. You're not bad at love; you're just someone learning to trust safety again.

Love Doesn't Wait for "Fully Healed"

The idea that you have to be completely healed before you can love is adorable, and also false. That's like waiting until you're in perfect shape to join a gym.

Healing happens through relationship: every healthy connection is a small retraining of your nervous system that whispers, "See? It's safe to connect."

You don't need to be flawless; you just need to be honest.

Tell the truth about what you need.

Admit when your energy is low.

That's intimacy, too.

Boundaries Are Romantic (Actually)

Setting boundaries isn't a rejection of love; it's an invitation to sustainable love. Saying, "I need a moment," or "That topic's a bit much right now," is not emotional sabotage, it's emotional hygiene.

Healthy love doesn't require you to be endlessly available. It thrives when both people can take turns being human.

When Old Wounds Show Up Mid-Hug

Sometimes the past barges into the present like an uninvited party guest.

A tone of voice, a facial expression, even kindness can stir up old alarm bells.

When that happens, try this: pause, breathe, name it.

"Hey, I'm feeling triggered right now. It's not about you; my body's just remembering something."

If you're with someone safe, they'll understand. If they don't, well, that's useful data too.

You Can Be a Work in Progress and Still Love Beautifully

Loving while healing means sometimes needing to retreat, sometimes needing to reach out.

It means apologizing when you misfire, forgiving yourself when you freeze, and celebrating tiny moments of connection that once felt impossible.

You don't have to be "ready." You just have to be real.

Healing doesn't disqualify you from love. It deepens your capacity for it.

You can care for others and yourself at the same time.

You can hold love and boundaries in the same breath.

You can be messy, brave, and learning, and still be worthy of joy.

Because loving while healing isn't about perfection, it's about letting your heart practice safety in real time.

Chapter 10: When It's Hard to Love Someone Who's Been Hurt

Loving someone with trauma isn't about tiptoeing on eggshells.

It's about learning to dance around the occasional landmine, with grace, humor, and maybe snacks.

When you love someone with trauma, it's important to understand that *trauma doesn't have a single face.*

It doesn't always come from the most visible or "difficult" situations.

Trauma can come from neglect, exposure to combat, emotional invalidation, sudden loss, chronic stress, abuse, recurring deployments, instability, or even the quiet absence of safety over time. And because the roots of trauma vary so widely, the ways it shows up in people do too.

Some wounds scream. Others whisper.

But all of them leave their mark on the nervous system, shaping how someone experiences the world and how they protect themselves.

There's no right or wrong way to respond to being traumatized, only the body's attempt to feel safe again.

Loving someone who carries trauma can feel like trying to care for a house with faulty wiring.

Sometimes the lights flicker without warning.

Sometimes the whole system shuts down.

You might say something completely neutral, only to be met with silence, fear, or frustration.

You might feel like you're walking on eggshells over invisible landmines.

And it's not because they don't care or don't love you.

It's because their body learned, somewhere along the way, that even love could be risky.

Sometimes, love isn't about fixing, rescuing, or making someone lean on you.

For many who've been hurt, being loved feels safest when it honors their independence. It's about showing up without expectation, without pressure, and without the need to "take care" of everything.

It's about being steady, patient, and present, allowing them to simply be themselves, free to choose, free to feel, and free to exist without having to rely on anyone else for their sense of safety or worth. That quiet kind of love can be the most powerful of all.

Loving someone with trauma is like tending to a sunflower garden that's learned to grow through concrete.

The flowers are real.

You just have to move slowly enough not to startle the roots

PART III:
THE MIRROR

Chapter 11: Emotional Inconsistency and the Nervous System's Alarm

One of the most misunderstood experiences for trauma survivors is how *tiny emotional shifts* can feel like *massive emotional earthquakes.*

A text reply takes a little longer than usual.

Someone's tone sounds slightly different.

A friend seems a bit distant.

Logically, you know it could mean nothing. Emotionally, it feels like everything.

Your chest tightens, your brain spins, and suddenly you're wondering what you did wrong, as if you've been dropped into a silent alarm system that only you can hear.

This isn't because you're needy, dramatic, or "too sensitive."

It's because, for you, inconsistency once meant danger.

When Inconsistency Meant Survival

If you grew up in a home where love was unpredictable, warm one moment, cold the next, your nervous system learned a painful truth: *pay attention or get hurt.*

A parent's silence might have meant punishment.

A change in mood could have meant rejection.

A small frown might have been the start of an explosion.

So now, even as an adult, your body treats inconsistency like an incoming storm. It starts scanning for clues, rehearsing worst-case scenarios, and preparing for impact.

It's not your mind being irrational. It's your *body being loyal.*

It's protecting you the only way it knows how.

The Brain's Old Programming

Here's the funny (and exhausting) part: your nervous system doesn't have a "modern update." It can't tell the difference between a delayed text and emotional abandonment.

It just sees "uncertainty" and shouts, *"Emergency! Something's wrong!"*

Meanwhile, your rational brain is over here trying to calm things down like, "Hey, maybe they're busy and haven't checked their phone?"

And your body goes, "Sure, but what if that's just a metaphor for rejection?"

This internal tug-of-war isn't proof that you're broken; it's evidence that your body is still trying to keep you safe using old data.

When the Alarm Sounds

When emotional inconsistency triggers that familiar panic, it's easy to spiral into shame: *"Why am I like this?"*

Try swapping that question for a gentler one: *"What part of me feels unsafe right now?"*

That shift turns judgment into curiosity, and curiosity is the first step toward regulation.

Then, instead of chasing reassurance from others (which can help but won't fix the root), try grounding yourself back into the present.

Small grounding cues can reset the alarm:

- Feel your feet on the ground.

- Take a slow exhale that's longer than your inhale.

- Say out loud: *"This feels familiar, but I'm safe right now."*

The goal isn't to silence your body. It's to teach it new evidence: *not every pause means danger anymore.*

The Healing Practice

Emotional consistency is safety in action.

It's showing up when you say you will.

It's staying kind when communication gets messy.

It's giving your nervous system, and others', time to realize that not every change is a threat.

The work isn't to eliminate your reactions. It's to slowly rewire your body to believe: *"I can feel uncertain and still be safe."*

That's where freedom begins, not in perfect control, but in calm self-trust.

Healing isn't about never being triggered. It's about learning to turn off the alarm when you realize there's no fire.

Chapter 12:
Triggers in Daily Life

What to do when trauma shows up at work, with friends, or when you're just trying to drink your coffee in peace.

Healing doesn't mean you'll never get triggered again. It just means when your nervous system freaks out, you know how to offer it a cup of tea instead of a lecture.

Healing isn't the end of triggers; it's learning how to respond when they knock on your door.

And yes, sometimes they knock at the *worst* times.

During a work meeting.

Mid-text with a friend.

In the middle of what was supposed to be a peaceful afternoon, where your only plan was "do nothing and breathe."

Triggers don't ask for appointments; they just show up, uninvited and overconfident.

But here's the truth: being triggered doesn't mean you've regressed. It means your body still cares deeply about keeping you safe.

Normalize the Presence of Triggers

You can be *safe* and still *feel unsafe.*

That's not failure, it's biology.

Your nervous system is like a loyal guard dog that hasn't quite realized you've moved to a safer neighborhood.

It barks at passing joggers, mailmen, and occasionally your own shadow, not because it's bad, but because it remembers when the world wasn't trustworthy.

So instead of judging yourself for being triggered, try this mindset: *"Oh, hey, my body's having a moment. Thanks for trying to protect me, but we're okay now."*

That small shift, from shame to awareness, is the heartbeat of healing.

Common Situations: Where Triggers Love to Hide

At Work

Workplace triggers often revolve around control, criticism, or power dynamics.

Someone raises their voice.

You get unexpected feedback.

The phrase "we need to talk" makes your stomach drop like you just got called to the principal's office.

Remember: your body isn't reacting to your boss, it's reacting to the *memory* of what being powerless once felt like.

When you feel yourself spiraling, take a slow breath, uncross your arms, and plant your feet.

Grounding in your body brings you back to *this* moment, not the one your nervous system is replaying.

With Friends

Being left out, misunderstood, or dismissed can light up old wounds fast.

Maybe you find yourself over-explaining, apologizing, or withdrawing altogether.

Here's the reminder: not every silence is rejection, and not every pause means punishment.

If something stings, you're allowed to name it gently: *"When plans change without me, it brings up old stuff for me. I know it's not intentional, but I wanted to share that."*

That's not neediness, that's emotional fluency.

When You're Alone

Ah, the solo trigger, the quiet asshole that sneaks in through unstructured time.

No meetings.

No distractions.

Just you, your thoughts, and that one memory that apparently set a Google Calendar reminder to show up *right now*.

Maybe your thoughts get loud.

Maybe the room feels too quiet.

Maybe you start doom-scrolling or cleaning the kitchen as it owes you money.

Being alone can unearth the echoes of old loneliness, not just the absence of people, but the absence of safety.

For trauma survivors, silence can feel suspicious. The nervous system goes, *"We've seen this movie before, and it didn't end well."*

When this happens, remember: silence isn't emptiness; it's space.

It's not proof that you're disconnected; it's an invitation to reconnect with yourself.

Try grounding in sensory experiences:

- Light a candle or open a window, let the air remind you that life is still moving around you.

- Put on music that feels like home (bonus points if it makes you sing off-key).

- Wrap yourself in something soft; texture is language to the nervous system.

- Text someone kind, even just to say, "Hey, my brain's being weird." (You don't need to explain more than that.)

- Move your body gently, stretch, sway, take three steps in any direction, and call it a dance.

And if your thoughts spiral, you can talk back:

- *"I see you, brain. You're trying to keep me safe again."*

- *"We're not in the past; we're on the couch."*

- *"It's okay to rest without earning it."*

Sometimes the trigger isn't the memory itself, it's the belief that you have to face it alone.

You don't.

Even when no one else is in the room, you can be there *for yourself.* That's not loneliness; that's reparenting in real time.

So light the candle.

Play the song.

Breathe into the space.

And remember: being alone doesn't mean you're abandoned, it means you're in the sacred company of your own becoming.

The Pause Practice

Before reacting, practice pausing. Not forever, just for a breath or two.

The pause is where power lives.

It's the difference between reacting *to* the wound and responding *to* the moment.

Try this:

1. Notice what's happening in your body (heart racing, stomach tightening, jaw clenching).

2. Name it: *"This is activation."*

3. Breathe. Don't fix, just notice.

4. Ask: *"What do I need right now, safety, space, or support?"*

Even a five-second pause can reroute an entire spiral.

Post-Trigger Care

After the wave passes, tend to yourself the way you would to someone you love.

Drink water.

Stretch.

Step outside.

Speak kindly to yourself, out loud if you can.

Some examples:

- "That was a lot. I'm allowed to rest now."

- "It's okay that this still affects me."

- "I handled that better than I used to."

You don't have to analyze every trigger. Sometimes you just need to *soothe the system.*

How to Communicate Triggers Safely

Naming your triggers doesn't mean blaming others for them. It means letting people know what helps you feel grounded.

Try:

- "I get overwhelmed when voices get raised. Could we take a breath before continuing?"

- "I shut down when I feel dismissed, and I want to stay connected, so can we revisit this later?"

This isn't "too sensitive." It's emotionally literate.

And if someone responds with compassion, celebrate that. You just modeled what safe communication looks like.

Being triggered doesn't mean you've failed at healing.

It means you've been given another chance to practice it.

Each trigger is a conversation between your past and your present, and every time you pause, breathe, and choose kindness, you're teaching your body a new story:

This moment is different.

I am safe now.

I can stay.

Trigger Care Toolkit - *A gentle survival kit for real-world overwhelm.*

The Three-B Rule: Breathe → Body → Belonging

1. Breathe: Inhale slowly for 4, exhale for 6. (The longer exhale tells your body: "We're not being chased.")

2. Body: Notice one physical sensation that feels neutral or good, feet on the floor, fabric on skin, or a sip of water.

3. Belonging: Remind yourself: *I'm not alone. I belong in this moment, in this world, even when I feel off.*

Five-Sense Grounding (if you've read my first book, you already know)

When your mind time-travels to past danger, bring it home through the senses:

- 5 things you can see

- 4 things you can touch

- 3 things you can hear

- 2 things you can smell

- 1 thing you can taste (coffee counts; so does gum. Or bad breath. I don't judge.)

You're literally teaching your brain: *We're here, not there.*

Self-Talk That Actually Helps

Skip the pep talks that sound like motivational posters. Try these instead:

- "This feeling is temporary."

- "My body remembers danger, but I'm safe right now."

- "I can feel this and still function."

- "I don't have to figure it all out this minute."

- "Even if this is messy, I'm doing better than I used to."

Micro-Soothing Moves

Small things, big calm:

- Run cool or warm water over your hands.

- Step outside and name one thing that's alive (tree, bird, overachieving weed).

- Stretch your jaw, roll your shoulders, unclench your toes.

- Play a 30-second song snippet that makes your nervous system sigh with relief. (Alexa, play "Higher" by Creed)

After-Care Journal Prompts

When you're ready, jot down a few lines:

- *What triggered me?*

- *What did I need in that moment?*

- *What helped me come back?*

- *What can I remind myself next time?*

This isn't homework; it's evidence of progress.

The 24-Hour Rule

After a big trigger, postpone major decisions or deep conversations for 24 hours.

Clarity loves a calm nervous system.

Drama loves a dysregulated one.

If You're Supporting Someone Else

- Stay calm; don't mirror panic.

- Offer grounding cues ("Let's breathe together," not "What's wrong with you?").

- Ask, "Do you want help or space?"

- Remember: You're a companion, not a cure.

Chapter 13: Communication That Doesn't Trigger

Listen beneath the words.

Communication can be connection, or it can be collision.

For people living with trauma, and for those who love them, even simple conversations can feel like walking through a minefield. A single tone of voice, a pause too long, a sudden change in facial expression, any of these can activate the nervous system, sending the body into fight, flight, freeze, or fawn before either person realizes what's happening.

The goal of trauma-informed communication isn't to walk on eggshells. It's to create an environment where both people can stay *regulated* enough to stay *connected*.

This chapter is about learning how to talk and listen in ways that build safety, not threat.

Tone, Timing, and Trust

The way something is said often matters more than what is said.

A calm tone tells the nervous system, *I'm not in danger*. A sharp or sarcastic tone, even if unintentional, can say the opposite. When someone has a trauma history, their brain is finely tuned to detect danger in micro-signals: raised eyebrows, tension in the jaw, crossed arms, a shift in volume.

Tone:

When possible, aim for gentle firmness, grounded but not harsh, steady but not cold. You can be direct without being aggressive, and kind without being avoidant.

A good rule of thumb: *Speak in the tone you'd want to hear if you were scared.*

Timing:

Timing is just as critical. Trauma survivors often need time to process before talking about something difficult. Trying to resolve conflict in the heat of activation rarely works; the conversation becomes about survival, not understanding.

If you notice tension rising, it's okay to pause and say,

"I want to talk about this, but I don't want to say things I'll regret. Can we come back to it when we're both calmer?"

That pause isn't avoidance, it's self-regulation.

Trust:

Trust in communication builds through consistency. It's not built by being perfect; it's built by being predictable.

Following through on small things, calling when you say you will, listening when you promise to listen, shows the nervous system, *I can relax here.*

Over time, trust shifts communication from *defense* to *dialogue.*

Listening to Emotions Beneath the Words

When someone with trauma communicates, the words you hear might not be the full message. A raised voice might really mean *I'm scared*. Silence might mean *I don't feel safe enough to speak*. Overexplaining might mean *I'm terrified of being misunderstood*.

Learning to listen beneath the words means tuning into the emotion and need underneath the surface.

Try responding to the emotion before the content. For example:

- Instead of: "You don't need to be upset about that."

  Try: "It sounds like that really hurt. Can you tell me what part felt hardest?"

- Instead of: "You're overreacting."

  Try: "Something about this feels really big for you. Help me understand it."

- Instead of defending your own intentions right away, pause and ask: "What did you hear me say just now?"

This approach slows down the reaction cycle and helps both people feel *seen*, which is the foundation of safety.

Conflict Repair in Trauma-Informed Ways

Conflict is inevitable. What matters most is what happens after.

For people living with trauma, unresolved conflict often feels like abandonment or danger. Repair is not about pretending nothing happened; it's about restoring safety through accountability and care.

1. Take Responsibility Without Shame

When triggers collide, both people might say or do things they don't mean. Owning your part, calmly and clearly, rebuilds safety.

"I see how my tone came across as harsh. That wasn't my intention, but I understand why it felt that way."

This separates responsibility from blame. You can take ownership without taking on all the guilt.

2. Regulate First, Repair Second

You cannot repair while dysregulated. If one or both people are still in fight or flight, the conversation will loop in circles. Step back, ground yourself, breathe, then return when the body feels safe again.

3. Use "We" Language

Shift from *me vs. you* to *us vs. the problem.*

"We got off track. How can we come back to each other?"

This small change in wording signals collaboration instead of combat.

4. Reaffirm connection

At the end of conflict repair, remind each other of what remains intact:

"I still love you."

"We're still on the same team."

"Thank you for working through this with me."

These affirmations anchor both nervous systems back into safety and belonging.

When You're the One with Trauma

If you're the person with trauma, remember you don't have to communicate perfectly to be worthy of love.

Sometimes your nervous system will speak louder than your words. That's okay. Healing means noticing when that happens and practicing compassion instead of shame.

Try to name what's happening in real time:

"I feel my body going into defense mode right now. Can we pause for a minute?"

This simple sentence turns a potential trigger into a moment of awareness, and that's powerful.

When You Love Someone with Trauma

If you love someone who's been through trauma, understand that their reactions are rarely about *you*. They're about *safety*. Your calm presence can be the difference between escalation and connection.

You don't have to fix their pain. You only have to help them feel safe enough to face it.

A simple question like, "What would help you feel safe right now?" opens the door to communication that heals instead of harms.

Communication after trauma is not about perfection; it's about presence.

It's about learning to slow down enough to hear what isn't being said, to speak from curiosity instead of defense, and to remember that every conversation is a chance to teach the body that connection can be safe again.

When we communicate with compassion, we don't just talk, we heal.

Chapter 14: When They Push You Away

Let's be honest, few things sting more than watching someone you love suddenly pull back.

They were open, connected, maybe even cuddly... and then *poof*, emotional ghost town. No texts, no warmth, just radio silence and vague "I just need space" energy.

It's confusing, it's painful, and if you're wired for connection, it can send your brain straight into panic mode: *What did I do wrong? Are they over me? Should I send a meme or a novel-length apology?*

Before you spiral, take a breath.

When someone withdraws after trauma, it's rarely about you; it's about their nervous system trying to survive closeness.

Their body isn't saying, *I don't care about you.* It's saying, *I care so much that it scares me.*

Why Trauma Creates Emotional Withdrawal

People who've lived through chaos often learned that connection comes with a cost.

Love wasn't safe; it was unpredictable. So, their body built a self-defense system: when things start feeling *too* close, *too* real, *too good*, alarms go off.

That's not emotional immaturity, that's a survival strategy.

Trauma can create freeze responses or dissociation. It teaches the brain: Distance keeps me safe. Closeness gets me hurt."

So, when they seem detached, they're not punishing you.

They're protecting the part of themselves that never got to feel safe being seen.

The Paradox of Proximity

Here's the paradox: the person who fears abandonment often dates the one who fears engulfment.

One craves closeness like oxygen; the other panics when someone gets too close.

Cue the emotional tug-of-war:

"Come here."

"Go away."

"Wait, why are you going away?"

It's not dysfunction, it's the dance of two nervous systems with different definitions of safety.

One feels safe in connection, the other in space.

And until both people understand that, they'll keep mistaking each other's coping for rejection.

How to Recognize Their Shutdown Cues

Avoidance doesn't always look like silence. Sometimes it looks like irritability, sarcasm, "I'm fine," or suddenly becoming very busy alphabetizing their spice rack.

Shutdown cues can include:

- Emotional flatness or disconnection
- Short, distant responses

- Irritation that seems out of proportion

- Wanting to be alone right when things start feeling close

It's not about manipulation; it's a protective reflex.

Their nervous system is trying to lower the emotional temperature before it burns.

Responding with Boundaries and Compassion

Your job isn't to chase or decode their every mood. It's to stay grounded in your own center. Meet their distance with steadiness, not desperation.

You can say, *"I sense you need space, I care about you, and I'll give it."* Then actually do it.

That shows more safety than any lecture ever could.

Boundaries aren't walls; there are doors that open both ways.

You can offer understanding without abandoning your own peace.

And when they're ready to reconnect, don't make them climb Mount Guilt to do it.

Just pick up where compassion left off.

What *Not* to Do

Don't take their distance as a personal failure.

Don't try to fix, chase, or force them to open up.

And please don't send seventeen check-in texts that escalate from "You okay?" to "Guess not."

The harder you push, the deeper they retreat, not because they don't love you, but because pressure feels like danger.

The goal isn't to pull them out of their shell. It's to make the world outside the shell feel safe enough to step into.

Chapter 15: Codependency vs. Compassion

Love deeply without losing yourself.

There's a fine line between loving someone and trying to *save* them, and most of us who grew up managing other people's emotions learned to sprint right across it.

Codependency often wears a beautiful disguise: kindness, loyalty, empathy, "ride or die" energy.

But underneath?

It's fear.

Fear that if you stop rescuing, they'll stop loving.

Fear that if you don't hold everything together, it'll all fall apart.

This chapter isn't about shaming that part of you; it's about finally understanding it, with the gentleness it always needed.

The Roots of Codependency

Many codependent patterns start early.

Maybe you were the *peacemaker*, diffusing chaos before it exploded. Or the *caretaker*, parenting your parents.

Or the *rescuer*, the one who could never let anyone suffer alone.

Those childhood survival roles don't disappear; they just grow up and start dating.

Suddenly, you're the partner who apologizes too much, over-functions, or feels anxious when someone else has a bad day. You think love means *earning* safety, when real love means *sharing* it.

You weren't broken; you were trained to take responsibility for everyone else's peace. But you can unlearn that. Like now. Please.

What Compassion Looks Like

Compassion is not codependency with better lighting.

True compassion feels like, *"I care about your pain, and I trust you to handle it."*

It's empathy with boundaries.

It's being present without performing CPR on someone else's emotions.

It's saying, *"I love you, but I won't rescue you at the expense of myself."*

Compassion honors both hearts, theirs and yours.

Recognizing Over-functioning

If you're constantly exhausted, anxious, or secretly resentful in relationships… you might be over-functioning.

That's the emotional version of running around the ship patching everyone else's holes while ignoring your own slow leak.

Here's a simple check: If you're doing more emotional labor than love requires, it's not devotion, it's depletion.

Over-functioning looks like:

- Solving problems that weren't yours to solve

- Reading moods like your life depends on it

- Confusing "helping" with "controlling" (ouch, but true)

You can't pour from an empty cup, and if you keep trying, the people you love will end up drinking your burnout.

Healthy Interdependence

The opposite of codependency isn't isolation, it's *interdependence*.

Two whole people choosing to walk beside each other, not inside each other's nervous systems.

Healthy interdependence says:

"I want you, but I don't need to lose myself to have you."

"I can stand on my own, and I can still lean on you."

It's a connection without captivity.

Love without self-erasure.

It's the space where trust grows because freedom is allowed.

The Practice of Letting Others Struggle

This is the hardest part: letting people struggle.

If you've spent your life rescuing others, watching someone you love hurt can feel unbearable. But sometimes, loving them means stepping back.

Because every time you save someone from their pain, you also save them from their growth.

Letting go isn't cold, it's courageous.

It's saying, *"I believe in your ability to heal, even when it's uncomfortable to watch."*

That's not abandonment. That's respect.

Key Message: True Compassion Includes Compassion for Yourself

You can't offer sustainable love if you're running on self-neglect.

True compassion includes boundaries, rest, and the radical idea that your peace matters too.

You don't have to shrink to love big.

You don't have to fix to be worthy.

You can be kind and still say *no*.

You can care deeply and still choose yourself.

Because in the end, the most loving thing you'll ever do for others is to stop disappearing for them.

Part IV:
The Healing

Chapter 16:
Building a Trauma-Informed Relationship

If relationships are a dance, then trauma adds a few surprise steps, like tripping over your own feet, accidentally elbowing your partner, and then apologizing twelve times while checking if they're mad.

A trauma-informed relationship isn't about being perfect; it's about being aware.

It's love with its eyes open. It's saying, "Hey, I know you flinch when someone raises their voice, and I want to learn how to hold that with care."

This kind of love doesn't just happen, it's built.

Slowly.

Kindly.

Repeatedly.

Consistency and Safety as Love Languages

Forget grand gestures and surprise trips to Bali (though, to be clear, if someone wants to book that, we're not saying no).

For many trauma survivors, consistency *is* the love language.

It's the text that says, *"I'll be there at 6:00,"* followed by them actually being there at 6:00.

It's the partner who keeps their word, not because it's romantic, but because it's safe.

Safety doesn't always feel like fireworks, it feels like exhaling.

It's calm, quiet, and sometimes a little boring.

But when your nervous system has been living in survival mode, *boring is bliss.*

Small Repairs, Big Impact

Every relationship has micro-ruptures, those little moments of tension or miscommunication.

The difference in trauma-informed love is that we *repair* them.

Quickly.

Gently.

Without turning them into emotional murder mysteries.

Without holding grudges

"Hey, I noticed you got quiet after I said that. Did something land weird?"

Those 14 words can save a relationship.

You don't have to avoid mistakes; you just have to own them.

In trauma-informed love, repair isn't weakness, it's maintenance.

Think of it as emotional oil changes. Ignore them, and eventually, the whole engine starts smoking.

Creating Shared Rituals of Regulation

When the world, or your nervous system, starts to feel unsafe, shared rituals help bring things back into rhythm.

Maybe it's a nightly walk after dinner, holding hands in silence.

Maybe it's sitting in the car for five minutes before going inside, just breathing together like synchronized weirdos.

Maybe it's music, prayer, laughter, or that long hug where you both exhale and realize, *Oh right, we're on the same team.*

These rituals tell your body, "We're safe here."

And when you've lived through the opposite, that's not a small thing; it's revolutionary.

When Something Small Bothers You

Here's the thing about trauma: it can make small things feel enormous.

A tone of voice, a forgotten text, a slammed cabinet, boom, your brain is suddenly filing for emotional bankruptcy.

A trauma-informed partner doesn't say, "That's stupid, why are you upset?"

They say, "It matters to you, so it matters to me."

You don't have to *understand* why something bothers you person. You just have to respect it.

Because in a trauma-informed relationship, empathy > logic.

You can be right, or you can be kind. *Choose kind; it pays better dividends.*

Love Languages (and Why We Sometimes Do the Opposite)

Ah, love languages, the five-part personality quiz that's ruined countless couples' date nights.

But here's a secret: our trauma often flips our love languages inside out.

If your love language is *words of affirmation*, you might shut down compliments because they feel suspicious.

If it's *physical touch*, you might feel overwhelmed when all your child wants is to be held... like all the time. You might flinch when someone reaches out, because your body hasn't learned that touch can be safe.

If it's *acts of service*, you might refuse help because somewhere along the line, you learned that needing others meant weakness or expectations of a return.

Healing means learning to receive what you ask for.

It's realizing that your partner saying "I love you" isn't a trap, it's a gift.

That being cared for isn't control, it's connection.

And that love, when it's trauma-informed, doesn't just feel good. It feels *safe*.

A trauma-informed relationship isn't the absence of pain. It's the presence of awareness.

It's two people saying, "I see your triggers, I'll meet them with tenderness, and maybe some ice cream."

Because nothing says "I love you and I understand your attachment wounds" like showing up.

Chapter 17: When Both of You Have Trauma

Ah, the trauma duo. #TraumaBonding.

Two people, both with deep histories, tender hearts, and enough emotional awareness to fill an entire therapist's calendar.

When it works, it's magic, like two survivors finding home in each other's arms.

When it doesn't... well, let's just say it's a lot of "Wait, are you mad at me?" followed by, "I don't know, are *you* mad at *me*?"

When both partners have trauma, love becomes a delicate dance between empathy and overload.

You see each other so clearly that it's both comforting and confronting. You speak the same emotional language, but sometimes you're also reenacting the same painful script.

This chapter isn't about choosing between love and healing. It's about learning when to hold, when to step back, and how to keep the love alive while your nervous systems are still figuring things out.

Shared Understanding vs. Shared Dysregulation

When two people with trauma connect, it often starts beautifully. There's instant safety, shared depth, and that unspoken knowing, *You get me.*

It feels cosmic.

Soulmate-level.

But that same understanding can morph into shared *dysregulation.*

Empathy becomes entanglement.

You stop knowing where your emotions end, and theirs begin.

Suddenly, you're both spiraling, one person crying while the other Googles "how to emotionally regulate your partner at 2 a.m."

Here's the truth: You can understand someone's pain without absorbing it. *You can witness without fixing.*

Love doesn't have to mean mutual drowning, it can mean learning to swim beside each other.

How Triggers Interlock

This one's tricky, and almost darkly poetic.

Your trauma might not just clash with your partner's; it might *fit* with it.

The person who fears abandonment often finds the one who fears engulfment.

One reaches forward, the other steps back, and suddenly you're both reenacting your childhoods in real time.

When you catch yourselves in this loop, **pause.**

Instead of asking, *"Why are you doing this to me?"* try, *"What old story are we both reliving right now?"*

That question can shift everything, from blame to understanding, from chaos to curiosity.

Because the problem isn't that you're broken.

It's that your pain learned to dance, and now, it's time to teach it new choreography.

The Power of Co-Regulation

Here's where things get hopeful.

When two people learn to co-regulate, they stop being each other's therapists and start being each other's calm.

Co-regulation isn't "fixing" your partner, it's saying, *"Hey, I see your storm. Let's breathe until the lightning passes."*

It's the gentle hand squeeze during an argument.

The soft tone instead of the defensive one.

The hug that says, *"You're safe. I'm here."*

You don't have to heal each other.

You just have to create enough safety that healing becomes possible.

Conflict as Mirror

In trauma-informed love, conflict isn't the enemy, it's the teacher.

Each argument is like a mirror reflecting something unhealed in both of you.

Maybe your partner's silence hits that part of you that once felt ignored. Maybe your anger wakes up their old fear of danger.

When you stop seeing conflict as proof you're incompatible and start seeing it as a call to awareness, everything changes.

Instead of *"You're impossible,"* it becomes, *"Oh, this is where it still hurts."*

That shift turns fights into opportunities for repair, and honestly, that's where intimacy gets real.

When It's Too Much

Sometimes, love is deep, but the timing is wrong.

You can adore each other and still be too raw, too flooded, or too triggered to grow together right now.

Parallel healing doesn't mean you've failed, it means you're wise enough to know that space can be sacred.

You can say, *"I love you, but I need to stabilize my own nervous system before I can share it with someone else."*

Because the truth is: you can't pour from an empty cup. And if both of you are running on emotional fumes, love becomes survival, not connection.

Love Doesn't Fix; It Supports

You can love each other fiercely and still need space to heal.

You can be soul-deep connected and still say, *"I need a break to come back to myself."*

That isn't failure, it's maturity.

When two people with trauma choose awareness over reaction, grace over defensiveness, and curiosity over control...

They don't just *survive* love.

They *transform* it.

118

Chapter 18: When Love Isn't Enough

Love is beautiful.

It's powerful.

It can move mountains, inspire poetry, and make us believe in things we swore off after our last disastrous situationship.

But sometimes, brace yourself, it's not enough.

And no, that's not cynicism talking. It's wisdom, wrapped in a warm blanket of hard-earned experience (and maybe a glass of wine).

Red Flags vs. Trauma Responses

Let's get something straight: not every red flag means you've stumbled into the emotional version of a haunted house.

Sometimes what looks like a red flag is actually someone's trauma response waving its arms, yelling, *"I'm scared, not toxic!"*

That said, some flags really are red. Like, *Communist-parade* red.

The key is discernment, learning to tell the difference between "I'm triggered" and "I'm treating you like trash."

If you find yourself constantly making excuses like, *"They didn't mean to scream at me; they just had a bad childhood,"* it might be time to remember that compassion doesn't require self-destruction.

Love can understand the wound, but it shouldn't have to bleed for it.

Walking Away from Relationships That Harm

Walking away doesn't always look strong or sexy.

Sometimes it looks like crying into your pillow, Googling "how to stop caring about someone," and pretending to enjoy that self-care bubble bath that now just feels like soup for your body.

But walking away *is* strength.

It's choosing peace over chaos, self-respect over codependency, and healing over habit.

It's realizing that "we have history" isn't a good enough reason to have a future.

Leaving isn't quitting, it's graduating.

Healing Alone vs. Healing in Connection

There's a myth that healing means disappearing into a cabin with herbal tea, yoga mats, and deep, reflective journaling.

Sure, solitude helps, but sometimes, we heal best when someone hands us the metaphorical tissue box and says, "Yeah, me too."

Healing alone builds resilience.

Healing in connection builds trust.

The trick is knowing which one your heart needs right now.

If you're prone to losing yourself in others, solitude is medicine. If you've built a fortress around your heart and labeled it "boundaries," maybe it's time to let a few safe people inside. (You can still keep the moat. Just lower the drawbridge occasionally.)

"If This Is You…"

If this is you, the one who stayed too long, who loved too hard, who confused pain with passion, take a deep breath. You're not broken. You're becoming.

If this is you, the friend of the one who stayed too long, don't lecture them. Offer empathy, snacks, and the reminder that they deserve gentle love.

And if this is you, the one still figuring out whether to stay or go, listen to your body. It often knows the truth before your heart catches up. Anxiety isn't chemistry. Peace isn't boring.

Sometimes, love isn't enough.

But self-respect, safety, laughter, and the courage to choose yourself?

Those are.

Part V:

The Becoming

Chapter 19: The Myth of the "Healed" Person

There's a quiet myth many of us carry in the back of our minds, this idea that one day, we'll finally "arrive."

We'll wake up perfectly healed, stretch gloriously in the sunlight, and feel nothing but inner peace and maybe the faint aroma of eucalyptus.

Nothing will shake us.

Our past will sit neatly boxed in the attic of our minds, labeled, sorted, and gathering only a polite amount of dust. We'll be ready for perfect love, perfect peace, perfect life.

But that day never comes.

And that's not because you're doing healing wrong. It's because healing was never meant to be a *destination.*

Healing is more like learning to live with yourself on a road trip, sometimes singing joyfully, sometimes sulking about snacks, and sometimes wondering if you missed the exit 20 miles ago.

The Illusion of Arrival

Somewhere along the way, healing got confused with perfectionism.

We start to believe there's a finish line, a golden gate where a serene monk stamps your "Healed" certificate and hands you a green smoothie.

But healing isn't a test you pass or a badge you earn.

It's more like learning to live with your heart open, even when it's raining.

The illusion of "arrival" keeps us chasing an ideal that doesn't exist. It makes us question our progress, shame ourselves for setbacks, and wonder if we're broken because we're still *feeling*.

But feeling isn't failure, it's part of the adventure (and sometimes the blooper reel).

127

Healing as a Spiral

Healing doesn't move in a straight line.

It spirals.

You revisit old pain, not because you've failed, but because you're meeting it with wiser eyes.

Think of it like hiking a mountain trail that loops upward. You might pass the same strange rock formation, but now you're at a higher point, plus, this time you remembered to bring water.

That's progress.

That's healing.

The Social Media Trap

In the age of curated peace and pastel affirmations, it's easy to think everyone else has already *healed*.

You scroll past glowing reels of yoga on mountaintops and wonder why you're still crying into your cereal.

But what you're seeing isn't always healing. It's performance, or at least, the polished highlight reel.

Real healing looks more like ugly crying in your car, forgiving yourself mid-sob, setting a shaky boundary, and showing up anyway.

It doesn't always look good. But it always moves you somewhere good.

Real Healing Markers

So what does actual healing look like?

It's not about never being triggered.

It's about noticing the trigger and saying, "Ah, yes, my old friend," instead of diving headfirst into emotional karaoke.

It's not about never feeling down.

It's about knowing how to hold yourself when you do.

It's not about never making mistakes.

It's about offering yourself a gentle "whoops" instead of a three-hour roast session in your head.

You become less reactive, more curious. Less self-critical, more self-compassionate.

And slowly, that inner voice that once sounded like a cranky sports commentator starts to sound more like your favorite supportive friend, the one who brings you tea and says, "You're doing amazing, truly."

The Wine Glass Metaphor

Imagine holding a wine glass full of red wine.

This wine symbolizes your pain, your past, your "stuff."

Now place that glass under a faucet of running clean water.

At first, it looks chaotic, like you're just making really bad sangria.

But as the water keeps flowing, the red lightens, then clears.

That's healing.

It's not instant. It's not tidy.

But with time, presence, and love, the clarity comes.

Not because the pain never happened, but because it no longer colors everything you see.

Living as a Work-in-Progress

You are not a project to be completed.

You're more like a garden, sometimes blooming, sometimes weeding, sometimes just lying there in the sun, unapologetically doing nothing.

You're allowed to be both a masterpiece and a work-in-progress.

You don't need to be "finished" to deserve peace. You don't need to be perfectly healed to be worthy of love (spoiler: you already are).

Real growth is showing up with your cracks, your quirks, and letting light shine through anyway.

You Are Not Unfinished; You Are Unfolding

Like a flower opening to the sun, sometimes gracefully, sometimes awkwardly sideways, your healing reveals itself petal by petal.

Every part of you, even the crumpled bits, is sacred.

You are not behind.

You are not broken.

You are not unfinished.

You are unfolding.

And you're doing it beautifully, even if you spill a little wine along the way.

Chapter 20:
Hope After the Wound

Integration, not erasure. Growth, not perfection.

Healing doesn't mean you never flinch again. It means you know what to do when you do.

It's not about erasing the past; it's about weaving it into something that no longer bleeds when you touch it.

The wound becomes a doorway. The scar becomes a story. And the person you've become on the other side? Someone softer, wiser, stronger, not because you avoided pain, but because you met it and kept going.

What Growth Can Look Like

Growth isn't always glamorous.

Sometimes it looks like not sending the text you would've sent six months ago.

It's saying "no" without a five-paragraph apology.

It's catching yourself mid-trigger and whispering, *"Not this time."*

It's also letting people love you in ways that feel foreign but safe, and actually letting it land.

Growth is messy, subtle, and wildly brave.

It's not about never falling apart; it's about knowing how to put yourself back together with kindness instead of panic.

Integration, Not Erasure

You don't have to delete who you were to become who you are.

Healing isn't a before-and-after photo; it's a collage.

Every version of you belongs here: the one who survived, the one who numbed out, the one who still gets scared sometimes.

Integration means your past doesn't run the show anymore, but it still gets a seat in the audience.

It means you can look back without living there.

It means your story no longer controls you; *you hold the pen now.*

Love That Feels Safe (Even When It's Imperfect)

Here's the thing: safe love isn't love without conflict. It's love without fear.

It's not the absence of discomfort; it's the presence of repair.

It's the gentle, steady rhythm of *"We're both human, but we're not going anywhere."*

Safe love isn't about finding someone who never triggers you; it's about finding someone who wants to understand what does, and learning to understand theirs.

It's hugs that calm your nervous system instead of confusing it.

It's being able to exhale in someone's presence.

It's laughter that doesn't cost you safety.

It's imperfect, and that's what makes it real.

If This Is You...

If this is you, the one who's still afraid to trust, still learning how to rest without guilt, you're doing it right. Healing isn't fast. It's faithful.

If this is you, the loved one walking beside a survivor, thank you for your patience, your curiosity, your quiet consistency. That's what safety looks like.

And if this is you, the one who isn't sure you'll ever get there, listen closely: you already are.

Every time you pause instead of panic, breathe instead of blame, stay instead of shut down, that's hope in motion.

The Gentle Truth

You don't have to become your "highest self."

You just have to be a little more honest, a little more kind, and a little more you than yesterday.

Healing won't make you perfec; it'll make you *whole.*

And wholeness isn't the absence of wounds; it's the peace of knowing you can live beautifully with them.

So, here's to the ones still patching up their hearts, still learning how to dance with their scars.

You've made it through the dark, not spotless, but shining anyway.

That's not the end of your story.

That's the light after the wound.

You matter;

Epilogue: You Made It Here

If you've made it to this page, pause.

Breathe.

Let that sink in.

You've just read an entire book about healing, heartbreak, trauma, and love, and you're still here. Still curious. Still open.

That alone is extraordinary.

Healing isn't for the faint of heart.

It's for the ones who keep showing up, even when it's messy, even when it's not Instagram-worthy, even when it feels like nothing's changing. It's for the ones who cry in therapy, cancel therapy, and then go back again because they refuse to give up on themselves.

If this journey has felt heavy at times, it's because you've been carrying a lot, and you finally started setting it down.

That's what healing does.

It doesn't erase the weight; it teaches you how to hold it differently.

You've learned that boundaries don't make you cold.

That softness isn't weakness.

That rest counts as progress. You're still strong, even if you're standing still.

That love, real love, can exist alongside fear, as long as there's awareness.

And maybe, most importantly, you've learned that you were never broken, just protecting yourself the only way you knew how.

So if you're tired, rest.

If you're hopeful, savor it.

If you're scared, that's okay too; growth always feels a little like stepping into the unknown.

You don't have to have it all figured out. You just have to keep choosing yourself, gently, repeatedly, imperfectly.

This isn't the end of your story. It's just the part where you start living it with a little more truth, a little more ease, and a lot more grace.

You are your own safe place now.

And that, truly, is the greatest love story of all.

Resource Appendix

Support & Crisis Lines

988 Suicide & Crisis Lifeline – Dial or text 988 (24/7).

SAMHSA National Helpline – 1-800-662-HELP (4357) for substance use and mental health resources.

RAINN (Rape, Abuse & Incest National Network – 1-800-656-HOPE (4673) or online chat for sexual assault support.

Crisis Text Line – Text **HOME** to 741741 (U.S.) for immediate support.

Veterans Crisis Line – 1-800-273-8255 (Press 1) or text 838255 for veterans and active-duty service members.

Online & Community Resources

National Child Traumatic Stress Network – https://www.nctsn.org

Sidran Institute (Trauma Education & Advocacy)
– https://www.sidran.org

Psychology Today Therapist Finder – https://www.psychologytoday.com/us/therapists

Local Support Groups – Many hospitals, community centers, and nonprofit organizations offer trauma-focused peer support groups.

Self-Care & Supplemental Practices

Mindfulness apps: Headspace, Calm, Insight Timer

Journaling: Reflective prompts for processing emotions and tracking triggers

Grounding techniques: Deep breathing, 5-4-3-2-1 sensory exercises

Yoga or gentle movement: Helps release tension and regulate the nervous system

About the Author

Kenzie is an Air Force veteran whose life journey reflects courage, resilience, and the power of healing. After serving her country, she faced some of her toughest battles within, navigating anxiety, depression, and PTSD. At her lowest, she struggled with suicidal thoughts and survived a suicide attempt, an experience that ultimately became a turning point rather than an ending.

Determined to reclaim her life, she sought therapy, embraced counseling, and remained open to the support of medication. Through this process, she discovered not only a path to wellness but also a deeper calling. Her diagnoses inspired her to pursue a master's degree in psychology, transforming personal pain into a purpose: to understand trauma, break stigma, and help both survivors and their loved ones navigate the complexities of healing together.

Wounded and Loving was born from that mission. Kenzie wrote this book for those living with trauma, and for those who love them, offering insight into the invisible wounds trauma creates and the relational challenges that often follow. With a voice grounded in compassion, lived experience, and hard-won wisdom, she invites readers into an honest conversation about healing, boundaries, empathy, and connection. Her hope is that these pages serve as a reminder that trauma does not have to define a person or a relationship, and that love and healing can coexist.

Today, Kenzie lives a life filled with love and meaning as a devoted wife and mother. She is happy, healthy, and passionate about sharing her story to remind others that recovery is real and no one is ever alone in their struggle.